HOUSES &
HOMES

TIM WOOD

HAMLYN

Acknowledgements

The publishers would like to thank Jonathan Adams who illustrated the see-through scenes; James Field who illustrated the cover; and the organizations which have given their permission to reproduce the following pictures:

Ancient Art & Architecture Collection: 20 top left.
Archiv für Kunst und Geschichte London Ltd/Erich Lessing: 15 top, 30.
Aspect Picture Library/Peter Carmichael: 27 bottom.
Bibliothèque Nationale de France: 27 top right, 28.
Bridgeman Art Library/Bibliothèque Nationale de France: 35.
British Museum: 8, 9 top, 38.
Cambridge University Museum of Archaeology & Anthropology: 9 bottom.
Domaine National de Chambord/Philippe Bricker: 31.
Werner Forman Archive: 15 bottom; right, /National Museum of New Zealand 37 left.
Robert Harding Picture Library: 5 bottom right, 5 top, 12 top, 12 bottom.
Michael Holford: 7, 10, 21 left.
Mansell Collection: 42.
Metropolitan Museum of Art/Rogers Fund & Edward S. Harkness Gift, 1920: 14.
Museum of London: 23 right, 23 left.
Museum of New Zealand: 36.
Scala: 21 right.
Science Photo Library/Peter Menzel: 44, 45 top, 45 bottom.
Science Museum/Science & Society Picture Library: 43 bottom.
Tokyo National Museum: 18.

Illustrators:
Jonathan Adams: Title page, 4-5 (small pictures),12-13, 14-15, 16-17, 24-25, 28-29, 32-33, 40-41.
Terry Gabbey (Associated Freelance Artists): 6-7, 8-9, 10-11, 22-23, 30, 35, 38-39,
Andre Hrydziuszko: 18-19, 26-27, 34, 36-37, 42-43, 44-45.
Kevin Madison: 4 (map), 34 (map).
Bill Donohoe: 20-21.
Richard Berridge (Specs Art): 31.
Richard Hook (Linden Artists): 46-47.
James Field: Cover.

Editor: Andrew Farrow
Designer: Cathy Tincknell
Production Controller: Mark Leonard
Picture Researcher: Jenny Faithfull

First published in Great Britain 1995
by Hamlyn Children's Books,
an imprint of Reed Children's Books,
Michelin House, 81 Fulham Road, London SW3 6RB,
and Auckland, Melbourne, Singapore and Toronto.

ISBN 0 600 58413 5

A CIP catalogue record for this book is available at the British Library.

Books printed and bound by Proost, Belgium

CONTENTS

HOUSES AND HOMES

The map below shows the locations of some of the main sites described in this book. The small illustrations show just a few of the many types of houses and homes that are built in different parts of the world and the great variety of building materials used.

In the last 3½ million years, humans have spread outwards from their original birthplace in Africa to colonize almost every region of the world. The earliest humans lived by scavenging and hunting. They were wanderers who built temporary shelters when they needed them. It is only comparatively recently, when humans discovered how to grow and store their own food, that they began to settle down and build permanent homes.

HOMES THROUGH HISTORY

The first homes were simple shelters. However, the development of farming about 11,000 years ago meant that people no longer had to wander in search of food. Farming was a much more efficient way of obtaining what they needed. People who farmed were able to live in larger groups and to stay in the same place all the time. As tools improved they began to build bigger and better buildings. Groups of people worked together to build stronger defences, more impressive palaces and finer temples to honour their gods. They began to decorate their buildings.

An igloo made of blocks of snow

Romany caravans, travelling homes in Europe

Crowded flats in Hong Kong

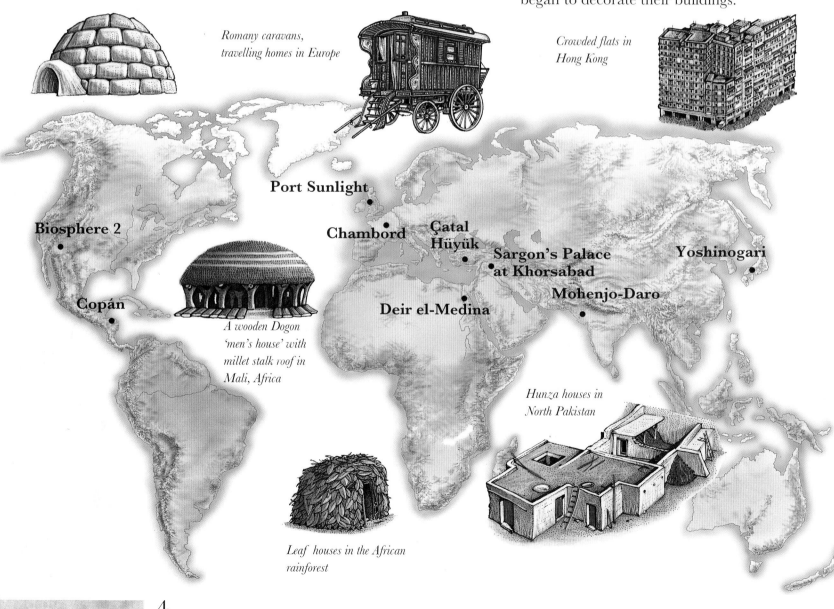

Port Sunlight

Biosphere 2

Chambord

Çatal Hüyük

Sargon's Palace at Khorsabad

Yoshinogari

Copán

A wooden Dogon 'men's house' with millet stalk roof in Mali, Africa

Deir el-Medina

Mohenjo-Daro

Hunza houses in North Pakistan

Leaf houses in the African rainforest

The soft rock found in valleys in Cappadocia, Turkey was hollowed out and used as shelters by Christians over 1,000 years ago. Paintings decorate the walls inside the caves.

DIFFERENT HOMES

People built different types of homes in different parts of the world. The types of homes they built depended on climate, what materials were available and their way of life. Climate has always been one of the chief influences on housing. People who lived in cold parts of the world designed their homes to keep in the heat and keep out the wind, rain and snow. People who lived in hot parts of the world needed protection from the sun, rain and insects.

DIFFERENT MATERIALS

Climate also affected the materials that people used to build their homes. In hot places where it seldom rains, mud hardened by the sun has always been a useful building material. In cold places people have had to use more permanent materials such as wood or stone. In tropical areas where vegetation is lush, and where it is very wet but cold is not such a problem, people have woven leaves to make rain-proof homes that were easy to repair.

DIFFERENT SHAPES

Climate also influenced the design of houses. In hot regions many people built their houses with small windows to keep the interior cool. Houses often had flat roofs, which were very practical in areas with low rainfall as they could be used as extra living areas. In swampy places or areas near rivers, people often built their houses on stilts to keep them out of the flood water. In cold regions people needed houses with sloping roofs so that rain and snow would slide off.

INDUSTRIALISATION

In the past, humans have sensibly built their houses out of the most abundant and easily worked local materials. For thousands of years, leaves, wood, mud and stone were the most widely used building materials. The advances in technology made during the 18th and 19th centuries have brought enormous changes to housing. Materials such as bricks, steel, glass, concrete and plastics are now produced on a massive scale and used in houses all over the world.

LIVING TOGETHER

Throughout their history, people have preferred to live together, in groups. They have deliberately built their homes on easily defended sites, near sources of food, water and raw materials, on trade routes or near places of religious significance. This book examines how, throughout history, humans living in different parts of the world have devised different ways of living together. In the following pages you can discover some of the rich variety of shapes and styles which people have used in the design of their houses and homes.

Houses on stilts are a common sight near the Mekong river in southern Cambodia. They are the safest form of housing in an area where the river floods each year. The water covers the fields with a layer of fertile silt.

A tipi (below left), a tent made by stretching buffalo hides over a framework of poles, was the home of the Plains Indians of North America. They could quickly pack up their tipis to follow the herds of buffalo they hunted. The concrete skyscraper (below) is now a common sight in most large cities where it provides high density office and living space.

About 18,000 years ago, huts made from mammoth bones and tusks were built at Mezhirich in the Ukraine. Few trees grow in this cold, windswept place. The bones and tusks of mammoths, killed by hunters with spears, clubs and pitfall traps, must have been the most plentiful building materials available. A typical hut was 5 to 8 metres in diameter.

Early Stone Age people lived by hunting animals and gathering fruits, nuts, roots, tubers and seeds. These hunter-gatherers had no permanent homes because their way of life forced them to move around, searching for food and following migrating herds of wild animals. They built temporary shelters as and when they needed them, or took refuge in caves.

LOCATION OF SITES

Hunter-gatherers chose the sites for their homes carefully. The best sites were near water, fords, supplies of raw materials such as flint for making tools and weapons, and natural passages for trapping herds of wild animals. In some places, hunters built their homes close to grazing grounds or migration routes. Many migrating animals follow regular migration routes so the hunter-gatherers revisited old camp-sites season after season.

These shelters, built by reindeer hunters at Pincevent in France about 13,000 years ago, were made from branches and the skins of the animals they killed. They looked very similar to the tipis of the North American Indians of the Great Plains of North America.

CAMPS

At certain times of the year, especially when the hunting was good, some groups of hunter-gatherers joined together and set up large camps. These were usually at the narrow mouths of valleys where they could intercept migrating herds. Many camps were close to rivers that provided drinking water and fish. Some of the group probably stayed near their camp most of the time, gathering food and fishing. Others hunted animals away from the camp.

BUILDING MATERIALS

To build their shelters the hunter-gatherers used whatever building materials were plentiful and could be easily gathered. The most common materials were branches torn or cut from trees, rocks, leaves and grasses. They worked all their materials by hand or with simple flint tools. In some places, the building materials came from the animals that were hunted, particularly hides and bones.

Life inside a Gönnersdorf hut. Horse hides probably formed the roof and walls of the shelter. The hides might have been made into clothes after the hunters had chewed them to remove the fat and soften the leather.

HIDE TENTS

Many Stone Age hunters used the hides of animals to make tents. We know from archaeological remains that one group of reindeer hunters camped on the banks of the River Seine about 13,000 years ago. They built oval-shaped tents, using branches and the skins of the reindeer they killed. Some of the hunters used flint scrapers to remove the fat from the skins. They stretched the hides to dry them, then sewed them together using bone needles to make clothes and tents.

SHARED HOMES

About 10,000 years ago, at Gönnersdorf in Germany, a group of hunters built circular tents using wild horse skins stretched over a framework of poles stuck into the ground. Each frame was strong enough to be left in place between visits. Many tiny crystal tiles engraved with simple figures of people, mammoths, horses and birds have been found buried under the floors. It seems that the settlement may have been occupied by two completely separate groups of people who lived there at different times of the year. One group lived in the tents during the winter. The other group, who may have been horse herders, lived there during the summer.

PORTABLE POSSESSIONS

Stone Age hunter-gatherers had to carry all their possessions as they travelled. They probably carried only what they needed for their immediate survival. Their most important possessions included weapons, tools such as flint scrapers and bone needles, and furs for warmth and bedding. They had no furniture and must have sat on the ground, on logs or on animal skins.

Reindeer provided not only meat and hides, but also antler. Antler was a valuable resource which could be carved into many useful objects, such as these harpoons for hunting fish.

CAVE DWELLINGS

This 14,000-year old needle-making kit was found in France. It comprises a grooved antler, a polisher, needles and stones for piercing.

The main living area was in the front of the cave. We know from remains in Stone Age hearths that 500,000 years ago our ancestors used fire for cooking and to harden the points of wooden and antler-tipped spears. At about this time, beds were made by filling pits with springy vegetation, and doors were made out of hides or woven twigs.

Almost from the start of the Stone Age, over two million years ago, people sheltered in caves. Huddled together, warmed and protected by fires, these early humans began to share conversations and dreams. This led to the first developments of religion and art.

CAVE SITES

At one time it was thought that all people who lived in the Stone Age were cave dwellers. We now know that very few groups were. This was partly because large caves, which are usually found in limestone rock, occur in relatively few places. Groups of hunter-gatherers soon used up all the food in an area. If people wanted to live in cave sites for a long period, they had to be near rivers or the sea which provided a constant and plentiful supply of fish.

THE ICE AGE

The main point of living in caves was to shelter from bad weather. Although the temperature inside a deep cave does not usually rise above 12°C, it will remain at about this temperature whatever the weather is like outside. Caves would have seemed comparatively warm places during the colder periods of the Ice Age. The inhabitants often made themselves more comfortable by building shelters in front of or inside the caves. Here they sat or lay on heaps of springy vegetation or animal skins which cushioned them from the rocky floor.

FIRE

Caves also gave shelter from the wind, making it easier to light a fire by striking sparks with flints and rock containing iron. Fire kept wild animals away as well as providing light, warmth and a means of cooking food. We are not quite sure when humans discovered how to make fire. Our earliest evidence shows that people living in China were using fire about 460,000 years ago. Cave dwellers also discovered that making a simple ring of stones, called a hearth, helped to control the fire and made the wood burn more efficiently. In many caves the hearth was placed near the cave mouth, in the natural light.

THE FIRST BURIALS

Some time between 100,000 and 50,000 years ago, people called Neanderthals began to bury their dead in graves under the floors of caves. Some bodies were buried singly, others in groups. Many were buried with some possessions, such as flint tools, and items of food. This is the first sign that humans had begun to think about a life after death. The tools and food would be needed by the dead to lead their new lives. Burial of close relatives under the floor of a dwelling has been a common feature of many societies since this time.

CRO-MAGNONS

As the Neanderthals died out, other humans began to flourish. We call them the Cro-Magnons. About 30,000 years ago, the Cro-Magnons began to carve and paint on their cave walls. Some paintings were simple hand shapes made either with a paint-covered hand or by blowing paint powder over the hand to make a 'negative' picture. Many paintings were of animals. It is possible that these had religious importance. Perhaps the painters believed their paintings would bring good hunting.

THE FIRST PAINTINGS

These Cro-Magnon artists achieved startling results with only the simplest of methods. They used natural bulges and dips in the rock to give their pictures form. Using only four basic colours, they painted with brushes made from animal hair or by blowing coloured powders, such as black charcoal, red ochre or white chalk, through hollowed out bones. Many paintings were created in chambers deep under the ground where there was no natural light. The early artists must have used burning branches or lights made from animal fat to see what they were doing. In some places they probably used tree trunks as ladders to reach ceilings and high walls.

There are over 230 caves, mostly in France and Spain, which contain paintings. The caves at Lascaux in France contain paintings of bulls and horses, the largest of which is 5.5 metres long. Maybe cave artists used a stone lamp like the one below, found in France. A wick would have been floated in animal fat in the hollow.

An antler skull and harpoons. The skull may have been used as a kind of helmet or head-dress, probably for ceremonial purposes.

HOUSES IN ÇATAL HÜYÜK

This 'Venus' figure found at Çatal Hüyük is almost certainly a fertility symbol. Mother goddesses like this are very ancient. They represent the creative power of nature. Their worshippers believed mother goddesses could give good harvests and large families.

Making bricks for a new house at Çatal Hüyük. Living in a house in Çatal Hüyük must have been like living in a cave. The walls of the finished houses were decorated with paintings and statues of fertility goddesses and animals.

About 10,000 years ago, some groups of people in the Middle East discovered how to grow crops and tame animals. Their wandering life was over. They settled down near their fields and built permanent homes. With more reliable food supplies and better homes, these first farmers now had time to learn other skills, such as weaving. They made new tools such as sickles for cutting cereals, querns for grinding the grain into flour, and pots for storing food. They also learned how to build strong stone walls and to make bricks.

THE FIRST TOWNS

Soon people began to gather into larger settlements for protection. They worked together to build public granaries, and traded their food surpluses with other communities.

The earliest town was probably Jericho, which was built in about 8000 BC. This important trading centre was defended by strong walls nearly 4 metres high and 2 metres thick. The town of Çatal Hüyük, which was built about 1,000 years later in what is now modern Turkey, had a different form of defence which may have been more effective.

ÇATAL HÜYÜK

The 6,000 inhabitants of Çatal Hüyük were Stone Age farmers and traders. They built their town near a river and used the water to irrigate their land. Each house at Çatal Hüyük was constructed around a strong wooden framework, the timbers of which were shaped with stone tools. The walls were built from mud bricks that had been made in wooden moulds and dried in the sun. The builders used mortar made of sticky mud to hold the bricks together. The walls were covered with a thick layer of daub - mud which was mixed with straw to bind it together.

A TOWN WITHOUT STREETS

Çatal Hüyük had very few open spaces and no streets. The houses were built next to each other, each one sharing its walls with neighbouring buildings. The inhabitants reached their own homes by clambering over the roofs of other houses. Once there, they went in though the main entrance, which was a hole in the flat roof, and down a ladder into the main room. The houses had no ground floor windows. Inside they must have been quite cool, although rather airless. The inhabitants had few pieces of furniture, but they regularly redecorated the interiors of their homes by painting the walls.

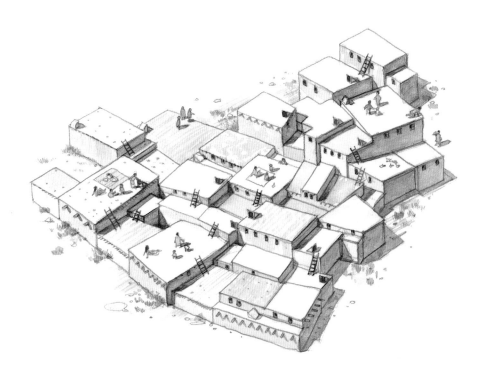

ORDER OUT OF CHAOS

At first sight the design of the town looks rather chaotic. Many houses were built on the ruins of earlier dwellings which had collapsed. This meant that roofs were at different heights. In fact there was a good deal of order and organization in the design. The bricks were made in standard sizes based on the length of the human hand and foot. Many of the houses were standard sizes too - about 6 metres long by 4.5 metres wide. Some details, such as doorways and hearths, were also very similar. Some of the open courtyards were used as places for leaving rubbish.

STRONG DEFENCE

The design of the houses was a useful form of defence. The rooftop entrances kept out wild animals. Although there was no perimeter wall as there was at Jericho, Çatal Hüyük was by no means defenceless. Once a wall is broken the whole town will probably be captured. But at Çatal Hüyük, attackers who broke into one of the outer houses would have been faced with a bewildering maze of other walls. Interestingly, while the famous Bible story describes the destruction of Jericho's walls, there is no archaeological evidence that Çatal Hüyük was ever captured.

This scene shows how the buildings at Çatal Hüyük must have looked. Remains found at Çatal Hüyük suggest that the town became rich through trade. A black rock called obsidian was one of the most important imports. The town may also have been a religious centre.

MOHENJO-DARO

This game board was found at Mohenjo-Daro. It appears to be for a kind of chess game. The fact that the inhabitants had time to play games like this indicates that their society was very wealthy.

Very little evidence of furniture and other household objects have survived from Mohenjo-Daro. The reconstruction of the house shown below is based on remains of the buildings and much guesswork about how the Mohenjo-Darans lived.

The straight streets, regular houses and evidence of a police force at Mohenjo-Daro suggest a well-ordered and highly organized society. The pierced pot (below) probably held scent and may have been used as an air freshener.

As humans improved their farming techniques, their communities grew larger. Along the banks of some large rivers, such as the Nile in Egypt and the Tigris and Euphrates in Sumeria, great cities developed. One of the best-planned cities was the Harappan city of Mohenjo-Daro, which was built near the Indus river in about 2000 BC. The city, which contained about 40,000 people, was very rich, probably because of the enormous wealth in grain which was stored inside its walls.

THE HOUSES

The lower part of the city was where most of the population lived. Most houses there were rectangular and up to 12 metres square. They had foundations and outer walls made of fired bricks held together with mortar. Fired bricks, which had been baked in large ovens, were much harder and longer lasting than sun-dried bricks.

The walls were up to 5 metres in height and were built around frames made from wooden beams. Regularly spaced recesses in the tops of the wall suggest that the beams slotted into the brickwork, helping to support the walls.

ACCOMMODATION

Many houses were two storeys high and large enough to hold a whole family, several guests, and servants. They were designed to be as cool as possible inside. They had few windows, most of which were covered with crossed bars or alabaster (a stone that can be broken into sheets) or terracotta (a form of pottery).

Many houses had open central courtyards, overlooked by rooms with balconies. These courtyards were probably used for domestic chores and as children's play areas. Only a few of the houses had outside windows, and most had just a single door which opened on to the street. These arrangements kept the houses secure, cool and free from dust.

HYGIENE

The people of Mohenjo-Daro probably kept their houses quite clean, because the city had the earliest known civic drainage system. Many houses had their own washrooms and lavatories. Fresh water was supplied to the houses by arched brick tunnels. Once used, the water was carried to the main city drains through gutters built near the walls of the houses. A network of earthenware pipes and underground drains carried waste water out of the city. At some crossroads there were places for dumping rubbish.

> **'Here may delight be thine through wealth and children...Remain here now, never to depart; enjoy the full measure of thy years playing with sons and grandsons. Be glad of heart within thy home.'**

— *A marriage blessing* —

THE GREAT BATH

The city also had a bathhouse. This was in the upper part of the city. The Great Bath may have been used for ritual cleansing during religious ceremonies conducted by the city's ruling priests. The building contains a sunken pool about 12 by 7 by 2.5 metres, which was made watertight with bricks, mortar and bitumen.

As with many ancient civilizations, there is much we do not know about the Indus Valley people. From the meagre evidence of ruins and a few objects, we do know that the civilization at Mohenjo-Daro lasted for over 300 years and then the city was abandoned in about 1700 BC.

Bricks at Mohenjo-Daro may have been made in kilns similar to this one (top). Bricks were piled in a beehive-shaped mound and a fire lit underneath. Finished bricks were laid in horizonal rows (above). The pattern of bricks in these rows is called a bond.

Gutters ran under the streets at Mohenjo-Daro, carrying water and waste away from the houses (far left). Brick toilets (the earliest known) were a feature of many houses (left).

13

AN EGYPTIAN HOUSE

A model of an Egyptian house. Models of buildings, people, work scenes and food were often put into tombs. They represented the real versions which it was believed could be used in an afterlife.

By about 3000 BC some cities had developed into powerful empires. One of the largest was in Egypt. The workers who made the pharaohs' tombs in the Valley of the Kings lived with their families, worked and died in a village built specially for them.

DEIR EL-MEDINA

Deir el-Medina was not a typical Egyptian village. It contained only highly-respected craftworkers who were much richer than the country's peasant farmers. They did not have to toil on the land, and they lived in considerable comfort.

The village was surrounded by a mud-brick wall 131 by 50 metres. Inside this enclosure there were 70 houses, while outside there were another 50. The houses were packed tightly together in terraces without gardens.

THE HOUSES

A typical house at Deir el-Medina was built in a similar style to houses in other Egyptian villages, but was larger. It was long and narrow, measuring about 10 metres by 3. It had rough stone foundations about 1.5 metres high, on top of which were walls made of mud bricks. The house had a flat roof supported by a large pillar.

The roof was reinforced by beams made from the trunks of palm trees. This framework was plastered with mud to make the flat surface of the roof. Each house had a single entrance which opened on to an alley. This may have been covered to protect the villagers from the sun. The doorway, which was painted red, was inscribed with the name of the occupant. The house had only a few windows in order to keep the interior cool.

INTERIORS

Most of the houses in Deir el-Medina were similar inside, with public and private rooms, an outside kitchen and at least one cellar. The internal walls were plastered and painted white. Some were decorated with paintings. The floors were made of hard-packed earth.

The villagers of Deir el-Medina were rich by the standards of the day. All the houses had flat roofs which greatly increased the usable living area. Can you see the oven in the kitchen on the left, and the shrine at the top of the stairs, below right?

'Do not let your conduct in the house be too high-and-mighty, and never lord it over your wife...Do not say to her "Where is so and so? Bring it here" when she has put it away carefully in some safe place.'

— Egyptian inscription —

The first room off the street was used for receiving visitors and for religious ceremonies. It contained a shrine at the top of a short flight of steps, where the women of the house made offerings. The second room was rather larger and usually lit by a high window. The main item of furniture was a built-in couch. Some houses had a shrine hidden behind a false door in the walls of this room.

PRIVATE ROOMS

Behind the two public rooms were two or more private rooms. These were used mainly as bedrooms, and contained headrests for sleeping on and storage chests. At the back of the house was a kitchen with all the things needed for preparing meals, such as grindstones, kneading-troughs, water jars and an oven. Many kitchens had a trellis roof which gave protection from the sun. Stairs led down to a cellar used for storage and, in some cases, as a family tomb.

A huge number of pottery fragments covered with hieroglyphic writing have been found at Deir el-Medina. This suggests that the inhabitants were much better educated than most Egyptians.

The Egyptians decorated their furniture with precious stones, ivory, metal and mother of pearl. Many Egyptian chairs had legs shaped like lions' paws. This chair, found in the tomb of an Egyptian queen, is also covered with thin sheets of gold.

15

SARGON'S PALACE

The see-through scene on these pages shows part of Sargon's palace. Most of the building was made from simple mud bricks. Harder, kiln-baked bricks were used to form archways and were glazed in different colours to create decorative panels. Wood from cedar, cypress, juniper and maple trees was used to make roof beams and gates. Part of the palace was dominated by a seven-tiered ziggurat which towered over the seven main temples, each dedicated to a different Assyrian god. The king took part in many religious rituals when he was in residence.

One of the most magnificent buildings of the ancient world was the palace of the Assyrian warrior king, Sargon II. Built as part of the new city of Khorsabad in what is now Iraq, the walled palace was truly fit for a king. It was nearly 400 metres square and contained 209 rooms. It was raised on a plinth so it towered over the landscape. The plinth and much of the palace were built of mud bricks. These were laid before they were completely dry, so that the whole structure solidified under its own great weight.

THE KING'S APARTMENTS

A series of courtyards, the largest of which was 28 metres square, divided the palace into three main areas - the king's apartments, the state chambers and a temple area. The king's apartments were luxurious. The floors were decorated with patterned pavements, although in many parts there were mats and even carpets.

When the king was not away at war, he enjoyed eating magnificent banquets. Some of the guests lounged on couches. Others sat on chairs and ate from tables. Servants fanned the diners constantly with large fly whisks made of woven reeds.

THE STATE CHAMBERS

The state chambers contained guest suites for visitors, such as ambassadors from other lands. The walls and corridors were decorated with stone reliefs and murals. These showed the exploits of the king, the Assyrians' victories, and the punishments given to their enemies. The murals were designed to impress and terrify visitors.

The palace had several bathrooms. Each contained at least one bath and a toilet. An Assyrian bath was a terracotta tub, big enough to sit in. Slaves heated the bathwater in bowls which stood on a hearth or brazier in a corner of the room. A chimney hood above the fire carried away the smoke. The toilet consisted of two raised foot stands with a drain between. The user squatted over the central groove. Brick drains, coated in bitumen to make them waterproof, carried away the effluent into underground sewage pipes.

THE ABANDONED PALACE

Sargon lived at the palace for only part of the year, resting from battle, receiving ambassadors and ruling his empire. As king it was his sacred duty to wage war against neighbouring countries. For most of the spring and summer, he was away on campaign. When Sargon was finally killed in battle, his son Sennacherib abandoned the largely unfinished city and its palace.

1 **Ziggurat**
2 **Temple of moon god Sin**
3 **Private apartments**
4 **Throne room**
5 **Royal apartments**
6 **Reception room**
7 **Bathroom**
8 **Sewage pipe**

The section of the palace shown below contained the state chambers and private apartments. The largest room here was the throne room which was 46 metres long. Here Sargon received important visitors and gave orders to his officers. Sargon's throne was raised on a stone platform.

The palace also contained a great many store rooms for holding the vast amounts of tribute sent by defeated countries. A number of rooms contained the thousands of clay tablets on which state records were kept. Scribes laboured almost constantly recording the king's words, and a number of offices equipped with clay benches were set aside for this work.

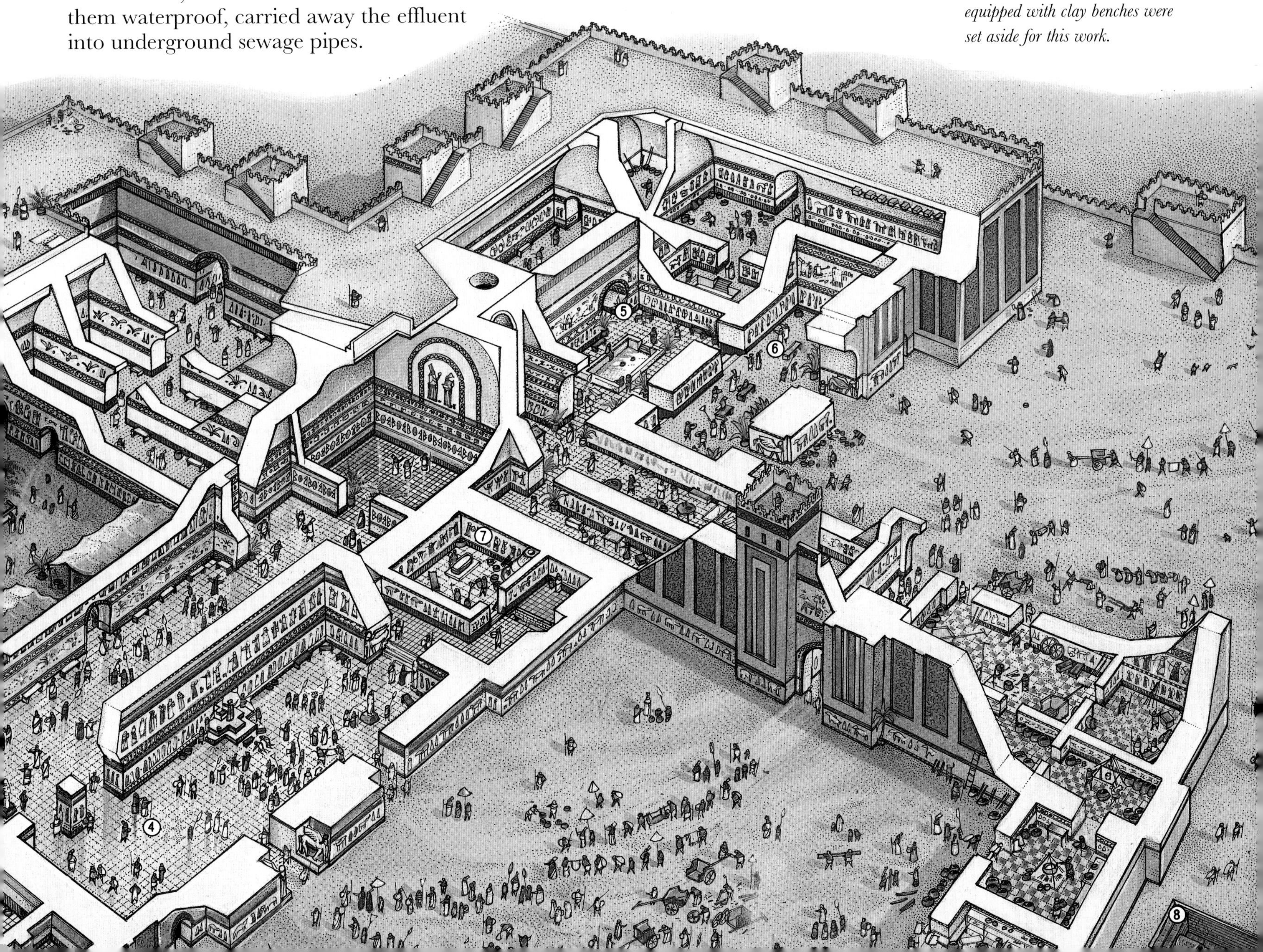

HOMES OF THE YAYOI

The Yayoi made fine clay ceramics. This elegant but practical pot was shaped on a potter's wheel. The neck is decorated with the mask of a human face.

Thatch provided a warm and waterproof covering for the roofs of Yayoi houses. Thatch is also safer if the roof collapses, as often happpened in this earthquake zone.

Protection from raiders was a high priority for the inhabitants of early farming settlements in many parts of the world. For thousands of years, walls and ditches were the most popular means of defending homes and the wealth of a settlement. The remains found at Yoshinogari in southwestern Japan, built over 2,000 years ago, show it was a fine example of a fortified farming village.

YOSHINOGARI

The inhabitants of Yoshinogari were Yayoi. These farmers were the first Japanese to live in permanent settlements. They grew rice and built villages near rivers and on the plains near the coast of Japan. The settlement of Yoshinogari was surrounded by a moat and a wooden palisade about 900 metres long. Around the edge of the settlement were several high watchtowers. This suggests that the Yayoi lived in troubled times. The palisade was obviously designed to defend the village.

THE BUILDINGS

Within the palisade, there were two main types of buildings - homes and storehouses. The oval houses were made mainly of wood and thatch, although some had stone walls. They were between 5 and 7 metres long, and 4.5 to 6 metres wide. Many of the houses did not have separate walls and roofs. Instead the whole building was supported on four sturdy posts.

The spaces between these pillars were filled in by beams bound with ropes. The whole structure was draped with a sloping thatched covering made of reeds which came right down to the ground. The shaping of the beams, and use of precise joints, show that the Yayoi used iron tools.

FLOORS AND WALLS

The floors of the houses were shallow pits dug in the ground. This type of floor is found in many parts of the world. In some places pits are used to save building high side walls. In other places they are dug down to a firm foundation for the floor.

The floors of some Yayoi dwellings were dug so deep that the inhabitants needed ladders to get in and out of their houses! The earth of the floor was beaten to make a firm surface. In the centre of each house was a clay fire pit. Around the edge of the house was a raised earth bench held together with wooden planks. This acted as a seat and also stopped ground water seeping under the walls.

OTHER BUILDINGS

Some of the houses were much larger than others, and may have belonged to richer people in the village. Although there is little direct evidence that powerful priests or rulers lived in the village, one grave found at Yoshinogari is bigger than the others, and might have belonged to a king.

Some of the buildings were raised on wooden posts and were rather taller than the houses. These were not homes but storehouses. Some of them had wooden collars fixed to the posts, to prevent rats getting at the rice and grain. Many had cleverly carved ladders leading up to the doors which were shaped to make it impossible for rats to climb.

Archaeological evidence shows that Yoshinogari (shown reconstructed below) must have had towers from where guards could watch the surrounding countryside to give warning of attack. The village suffered at least one attack because nearby are hundreds of graves containing the skeletons of people who met violent deaths, probably in battle.

Steps (top) may have been used to reach the storehouses. The shape makes it hard for rats to climb up. Accurate joints (above) helped to make the wooden walls strong and weatherproof.

LIFE IN A ROMAN FLAT

Roman plumbing was very advanced. The Romans had taps similar to the one shown here, water pumps and pipes. But only the richest people had water piped to their own houses.

Insulae were designed simply to accommodate as many people as possible in the least amount of space. In this block you can see the poorest apartments at the top, and the better flats and shops below

Ancient Rome and many other cities in the Roman Empire contained marble palaces, triumphal arches, stadiums and other impressive public buildings. But the glories of these buildings often hid the squalor of the tall apartment blocks and densely-packed slums in which most citizens lived. Many ordinary Roman citizens lived in cramped rooms in constant fear of fire, collapsing walls, muggers and other dangers.

ORDINARY CITIZENS

Nearly 70 million people lived in the Roman Empire. The richest owned majestic palaces or luxurious villas. Many had large gardens, running water, inside bathrooms, central heating, glass windows and beautiful mosaics and wall-paintings.

But most ordinary citizens could only afford to live in small apartments in tall blocks of flats called 'insulae'. There was no piped water or toilets, so people had to visit public baths to wash, and go to public lavatories. Water for cooking and drinking had to be fetched from the public fountains. Rents were high and people crammed into the small rooms to save money.

'But here...we live in a city that's propped up with matchsticks... That's the way the landlord stops the building from falling down, papering over the cracks in the old walls, telling us not to worry, to sleep easy and all the time the place is about to collapse around us.'

Juvenal

Insulae were heated with wood-burning braziers which were unpleasant to use because the flats had no chimneys. The insulae were crowded together and contained a lot of wood which created a fire risk. Most Roman towns had their own fire brigade, called vigiles. *In Rome there were seven brigades, each with 1,000 fire-fighters. The fire-fighters collected water from public fountains and pools in leather buckets. They also used small hand-held pumps, but these could not squirt much water.*

Lighting in Roman houses was provided by oil lamps made of pottery or bronze (like the one pictured below left). The lamps gave very little light, and we know that many Romans suffered with eye problems. Most Romans used chests to store their linen and clothes. Wardrobes, like the one shown below, were owned by the wealthy.

DEATH TRAPS

The ground floors of the flats were built from brick or stone held together with lime mortar. Above these were upper storeys built of wood and plaster supported by wooden beams and reached by steep wooden staircases. Brick arches were used for door and window openings. Most windows had shutters but no glass. Although there were some limits on the height of insulae - normally only five storeys were allowed - there were few controls over the actual building, and standards could be low. Often the cheapest materials were used. There are many reports of blocks of flats collapsing, killing and injuring the inhabitants.

SHOPPING ARCADES

In most Roman cities, the ground floors of the insulae were taken up with shops selling a huge variety of different goods. The shops were also workshops where the shopkeeper made the goods which were on sale. The upper storeys of the insulae overhung the ground floor shops and were supported on rows of columns which made a sheltered walkway for shoppers.

DANGER FROM ABOVE

The insulae had no drains or refuse bins, so people threw their rubbish out of the window into the street below. The poet Juvenal complained about the dangers which could come from these upper storeys, including falling tiles and pots. 'People will think you stupid', he wrote, 'if you go out to dinner without making your will first. Every open window can spell sudden death to the passer-by. So you just hope and pray they decide to throw out nothing more harmful than a brimming chamber pot.'

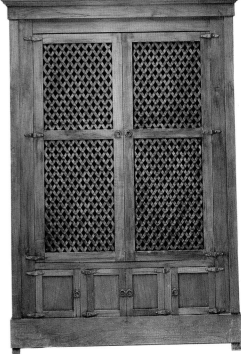

21

SAXON HOMES

No one really knows exactly what Saxon houses looked like. The scene below shows how Saxons may have built a house. In the background, workers are cutting radial planks. The pit was probably there to keep the floor timbers dry. We do know that the Saxons were skilled woodworkers who could cut complicated joints and who used pegs to fix wood together.

In the 5th century, members of many different German tribes, including Angles and Saxons, moved into parts of what had been the Roman Empire. Some of them settled in the Low Countries, while others crossed the North Sea and settled in eastern Britain.

WOODEN WALLS

The first Anglo-Saxons to arrive in Britain lived in villages. In some places, the Anglo-Saxons used stone from old Roman buildings to build their houses. In other places they added wooden extensions to existing Roman buildings. But in most places, the Anglo-Saxons built new houses out of wood which they cut from the surrounding forests. They felled the trees with iron axes and split the tree trunks lengthways with wooden wedges to make planks. 'Radial' planks made this way are much stronger than sawn planks.

Each building in the village was made from planks fastened with wooden pegs to a stout framework of wooden posts. The planks were slightly wedge-shaped and interlocked to form a draught-proof surface. Windows were simple openings which could be covered by wooden shutters in bad weather.

ROOFING

The Anglo-Saxons thatched their roofs with sedge or reeds which grew on river banks. First they put a light wooden framework on the roof, which was pitched to keep off the rain. Over this they laid bundles of reed stems cut to length. The reeds were held in place with hazel pegs called braunches. Thatch is an excellent roofing material which is still in use in many parts of the world today. It is light, waterproof and keeps in the warmth. There is no evidence to show that the Saxons had chimneys or smoke holes in their roofs. If that was the case, the interiors of their houses must have been very smoky. Evidence from skeletons shows that many Anglo-Saxons suffered from blocked noses which might have been caused by the smoke.

INSIDE THE HOUSES

Houses were often built so that their doors and windows faced south to maximize the light inside. Each house was built over a pit which was probably designed to keep the wooden floorboards dry. Inside, the furniture consisted of wooden tables, benches and stools. Beds were basically wooden boxes filled with animal furs and woollen blankets. A small fire in a sand-filled firebox provided heat and some light. At night they used candles made from animal fat. About 10 close relatives of all ages lived in each house. When the house became too run-down to live in, they simply built a new one in a different part of the village.

Waterlogged remains found in modern Germany prove that some Saxon houses had outside and inside walls made from wattle panels. From other remains we know that animals were kept indoors. Some houses had internal enclosures which could hold over 20 cattle. Most Saxon houses were roofed with reed thatch (right). Wooden shingles (below right) might have been split from straight-grained wood to make waterproof tiles for some halls.

FAMILY GROUPS

Each new village was home to several families who may have been distantly related. In the village each family group of about 30 people had its own hall which was a meeting place and where the family went to eat most of their meals. Around each hall were houses, used mainly for sleeping, and workshops which were shared by the family group. The workshops were used for weaving woollen and linen cloth and for other craftwork, such as carving bone and antler.

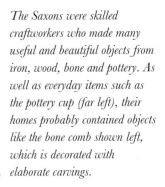

The Saxons were skilled craftworkers who made many useful and beautiful objects from iron, wood, bone and pottery. As well as everyday items such as the pottery cup (far left), their homes probably contained objects like the bone comb shown left, which is decorated with elaborate carvings.

23

HOMES IN A MAYAN CITY

The scene below shows two houses belonging to one Mayan family living in Copán. On the left is a sleeping house and on the right is a kitchen house. The Mayans spent what leisure time they had outside in the open air or in the ceremonial centre of the city. In many places where there was a shortage of building stone, including Copán, the Mayans also made the walls of their homes out of wattle and daub.

The Mayan civilization flourished in the Yucatan peninsula in Central America between AD 300 and 900. These mysterious people built great stone cities and worshipped exotic gods. Copán, one of the greatest Mayan ceremonial centres, contained huge pyramids and temples, and palaces where the ruling classes lived. However, most of the city's people were farmers who lived in dozens of villages scattered in the surrounding jungle. They came to the ceremonial centre only on market days or to take part in religious festivals.

THE HOUSES

Each peasant family had one or two houses which stood on a small plot of land surrounded by a dry stone wall. Houses could be round, square or rectangular, and were sometimes rounded at both ends. The building stood on rubble foundations and had a high pitched roof to keep off the heavy tropical rains.

The walls and roofs of the houses varied from place to place. In jungle areas, roughly shaped wooden planks or posts were commonly used for the walls, and palm leaves for the roofs. In highland areas, the sturdy walls were made with stones picked from the ground and stuck together with lime mortar. Roofs of thatched grass were common. The Mayans shaped all the building materials they used with stone or obsidian tools.

INTERIORS

Some families had two houses. They used one for sleeping and one for cooking and eating. Families with only one house divided it into two parts with a wall. Most houses had a single entrance without a door. The opening was hung with a curtain of string with copper bells tied on to give warning of visitors or intruders. The kitchen had an open fire on the floor. This was contained in a hearth made from three large stones which supported a flat ceramic baking dish. The smoke from the fire escaped through the thatch. At Copán, water was fetched from the nearby river in pots. Many other cities did not have a convenient river nearby, so the Mayans dug underground cisterns or built reservoirs to store rainwater.

THE SLEEPING ROOM

On the floor of the sleeping room stood low beds or sleeping racks, made from small branches laced together and covered with woven grass mats. The Mayans used the cotton cloaks they wore, which were called *mantas*, as blankets. They buried their dead under the earth floors of their houses, perhaps to keep the spirits of their ancestors close by. After several burials or when the house became too tumble-down to repair, the building was abandoned and treated as a sacred burial plot.

1 **Sleeping house**
2 **Bed**
3 **Kitchen house**
4 **Buried ancestor**
5 **Foundation made of rubble**
6 **Plastered stone walls**
7 **Thatched roof**
8 **Tomb in temple**
9 **Bees' nest provides honey**

The heart of Copán was a massive religious centre dedicated to the main gods of weather, crops and animals. In the centre of the city was an 'acropolis', a gigantic raised stone platform on which stood a number of important pyramids and temples. The Mayans probably used professional builders or even architects to build their temples, pyramids and palaces. We know they drew plans for some of their buildings on paper and wood. In contrast, the Mayans made no real effort to plan the outer parts of their cities. The houses of ordinary people were probably just built by family members helping each other.

25

LIFE IN A MONGOL YURT

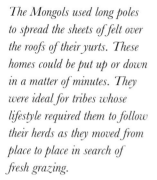

By about 1200, people in most parts of the world lived in cities, towns or villages. But one group of wandering herders living in Mongolia, known as the Mongols, hated city life and despised peasant farmers. At the same time they envied the wealth of the city-dwellers, and set out to conquer and plunder the rest of the world. Wherever they went, the Mongols took their houses - squat tents called 'yurts' - with them. They even chose their allies by whether or not they lived in yurts. Their leader, Genghis Khan, called himself the 'ruler of all tribes who live in felt tents'.

The Mongols used long poles to spread the sheets of felt over the roofs of their yurts. These homes could be put up or down in a matter of minutes. They were ideal for tribes whose lifestyle required them to follow their herds as they moved from place to place in search of fresh grazing.

NOMADS FROM THE STEPPES

The Mongol tribes were divided into 'oboks', or clans. Clan members lived in scattered family groups, each with its own grazing land. The Mongols' nomadic (wandering) way of life followed a pattern of seasonal migration. After spending the winter in sheltered valleys, each clan moved with its herds of sheep, horses and cattle to grazing lands on the high plateau of the steppes for the summer. As they needed to stay with their animals, the Mongols did not have fixed settlements. Instead, each family group lived in a collection of squat circular tents called 'yurts' or 'gers'. Their animals were kept in nearby pens at night or allowed to graze on the steppes.

YURTS

A yurt was made of a thick felt cover over a light frame of thin wooden struts. The floor was made of wooden planks, in the centre of which was a pole that held up the roof of the tent. Next to the pole stood a stove or firebox, for cooking and providing warmth, with a chimney that poked out through a hole in the roof.

For decoration and to help keep the yurt warm, rugs were hung round the wall. Arranged in a circle against the wall were beds, and the cupboards and chests that held the family's possessions and stores. The entrance usually faced south. This allowed the maximum amount of light in and kept out the cold Mongolian winds that blew mainly from the north.

ON THE MOVE

Yurts made ideal homes for nomads. They could easily be taken down, the felt rolled up and the framework dismantled in about an hour. But by 1200 many Mongols used large wooden carts to transport their yurts. Each yurt was lifted in one piece on to a cart. Mongol women drove the large teams of oxen which pulled the carts, standing in the entrances of their yurts.

While on campaign Mongol soldiers practically lived in the saddle, carrying all their possessions in leather sacks strapped to their horses. They ate mare's milk which had curdled in the sun. Their main drink was fermented mare's milk, called *kumiss*. Raw meat was often placed under the saddle of a horse to tenderize it.

AT WAR

The Mongols despised city-dwellers and often destroyed the cities they captured. When the Mongol armies poured into China and Europe, their yurts travelled in great hordes behind them, like fleets of ships carrying the families across the land.

In China, the Mongol leader Kublai Khan built a new capital city, then called Ta-tu and now known as Beijing. But even here, in the heart of the Imperial city, the walls of Kublai Khan's sleeping quarters were hung with carpets, rugs and silks so they resembled the inside of a yurt. Many important Mongol officials and members of the royal family preferred to sleep in yurts in the palace gardens, rather than in their official quarters.

Inside a Mongolian yurt. Although the furniture and possessions are modern, the interior of this yurt would have seemed very familiar to a Mongol living in the time of Genghis Khan.

TIMBER-FRAMED HOUSES

The builders often built sections of the frame in the woods where they felled the trees. At the site they assembled all the pieces and hauled them into position with ropes and pulleys.

A medieval upstairs toilet was just a seat with a hole in it.

During the Middle Ages, many houses were built using timber frames. Wood was plentiful and easy to work. The different parts of the frame, the walls, roof and floors could be joined together so that the whole building was like a giant box. It was a practical and effective design that became popular all over Europe.

MAKING THE FRAME

Timber-framed houses were made in sections so they could be put up quickly and easily. Oak was a favoured wood because it is very strong and resists rotting, and huge areas of oak forest were cut down. The craftsmen cut the timbers to length and shaped them using saws, axes and planes. They used different types of joints to connect the different timbers.

PUTTING UP THE FRAME

Once they had cut the timbers according to the plans they had made, the builders marked all the timbers so that they knew where each piece fitted. They carried the timbers to the site and fitted them together to make the sections of the framework. The timbers were locked into their joints with wooden pegs, called dowels, which fitted tightly into holes bored in the wood.

TOWN HOUSES

In towns, where space was limited, houses might have several storeys. In some towns the upper storeys of houses jutted out to give more floor space in upstairs rooms. This shaded the narrow streets below, making them dark and gloomy.

halved or trenched   *mortice (left) and tenon (right)*   *joint with holes for dowels (pegs)*

wattle and daub   *timber 'laths'*   *stone*   *herringbone brick*

Medieval builders made the frames using a variety of joints (top). Once the wooden frames were in place, the builders filled the spaces between the timbers. The most commonly used materials were wooden planking, bricks, wattle and daub, timber 'laths' covered in plaster, or plasterwork decorated with paint or swirling patterns, called pargeting.

Town houses often had space on the ground floor for a shop. The upper floors of merchants' houses were used to store goods. The kitchen was sometimes placed in a separate lean-to building at the back of the house to reduce the danger of fire.

WINDOWS

Only a very few houses had glass windows, which were expensive. They were made of small panes of glass, each of which had to be individually blown. The panes were kept in place by lead beading. Most people could not afford glass and had wooden shutters instead. These shutters, which closed at night, were used in the daytime as tables on which to display goods.

WASHING

Houses did not have running water or bathrooms. Toilet arrangements were simple. Some houses had outside toilets, called privies, which were small sheds over a hole in the ground. Other houses had toilets in small upper-storey rooms called 'garde robes' which hung out from the side of the house. Sewage fell through a hole in the floor on to a dung heap below.

COUNTRY HOUSES

In country areas, many houses had just one storey. A popular design for larger houses was the medieval hall. This consisted of a house built round one very large room with a massive fireplace which was used for heating the house and for cooking food. The ceiling of the hall was very high. Even so, when the fire was lit the room soon filled with smoke.

Chimneys were usually built of stone and, therefore, expensive. Only the grandest houses had them. It was not until the late Middle Ages, when bricks were made in large quantities, that chimneys became more common.

Timber-framed houses could be several storeys high, especially where they were built in rows so that each one shared a side wall with and helped to support the house next door. The house of a German merchant in the Middle Ages served as a workshop and storehouse as well as a home. Typically it had several storeys and was roofed with slates, tiles or thatch. The large pulley in the centre of the house was used for moving goods easily from floor to floor.

roof bay   *smoke hood*   *external chimney*   *internal chimney*

Changing fireplaces and chimneys in the Middle Ages from the earliest (left) where smoke from an open fire collects in a roof bay, to the latest (right) with an internal brick chimney. Chimneys carried smoke out of the house and made it more practical to add upstairs rooms.

Francis I came to the throne in 1515. He was a lively, boisterous, extravagant young man described by King Louis XII as a 'great boy'.

Royal hunts in the time of Francis I were stately slaughters. A vast army of huntsmen built a huge funnel-shaped trap of netting or sailcloth. Into this they drove large numbers of wild beasts, such as deer, boars and even wolves. The ladies of the court watched admiringly while the gentlemen massacred the animals with spears and swords, accompanied by music played by the court orchestra.

The valley of the Loire is one of the most beautiful regions of France. Along the banks of the river, French kings, princes and nobles have built dozens of castles. The first were forts, built by the dukes of Anjou to defend their lands from Viking raiders and English armies. Later, as life in France became more settled, the castles were designed more for pleasure than for war. Perhaps the most beautiful of these châteaux was that built at Chambord by King Francis I.

AN UNPROMISING SITE

The château was built in the heart of a dense forest full of shrubs, thorn bushes, heathlands and marshes. It was a solitary and melancholy place. But the area teemed with wildlife - deer and wild boar wandered in the huge park. It was an ideal site for a royal hunting lodge. Here, in 1519, Francis, who was passionately fond of hunting, began building the château.

FAIRY-TALE CASTLE

No one is quite sure who designed Chambord (see pages 32-33). The Superintendent of Works, Jean le Breton, was French, but the architects were probably Italian. The design certainly incorporates many Italian Renaissance features. Although the overall effect of the design is one of a splendid palace or fairy-tale castle, the plan of Chambord (above) is based on that of a fortress. It has a central keep, outer walls and corner towers, the whole protected by a moat. But the outside is embellished with a fantastic selection of turrets, gables, dormer windows, spires, lanterns and chimneys. Inside the rooms were decorated with pictures, tapestries and trophies glorifying hunting.

AN UNCOMFORTABLE HOME

Chambord provided a magnificent backdrop to the hunts, concerts, firework displays, receptions and balls which were organized to amuse Francis' glittering court. However, while outwardly splendid, the château was far too uncomfortable to be a proper home. Francis I rarely stayed at Chambord for more than three days at a time. The château could not be heated and was never furnished completely. It was abandoned before it was finished.

Dancing was a popular pastime at court, and there must have been great celebrations after a successful hunt at Chambord. During Francis' reign the galliard was very popular. This was a very vigorous dance with lots of leaping and thrusting out of the leg.

DESERTED AND BARE

Apart from the occasional caretaker, the château remained empty for a large part of its life, reviving only during the occasional royal visit. An inventory of furniture at Chambord made in 1685 records that the only furniture in the 400 rooms was one red velvet armchair, 30 ordinary chairs, some folding chairs, one red velvet couch, 18 stools, eight mirrors, six basins, four chamber pots, 40 chandeliers (18 of which were broken) and 13 tables.

IMPROVEMENTS

But Chambord was never quite forgotten. Later kings and other owners made improvements and added new buildings to the original. Maurice de Saxe, for example, converted one hall to a theatre with 1,800 seats. During the 18th century, it was occupied for about 25 years, first by Louis XV's parents-in-law and then by Maurice de Saxe and his entire regiment. Maurice spent a large fortune on the palace and lived there like a king. But in 1750 he died from what was reported as congestion of the lungs caused by the damp forest mists. (Others claim he was killed by a jealous husband in a duel.) Later, Chambord was looted during the French Revolution. After that its various owners were unable to repair the building. The château was bought by the French government in 1930. Since then millions of francs have been spent to restore it to its former glory.

This beautiful picture of Chambord is a decoration on a Sèvres vase ordered by King Charles X in about 1823.

One of the most beautiful rooms in Chambord was the bedroom of Marie Thérèse, wife of Louis XIV (right). The northeast corner of the château contains Francis I's bedroom and study, which were decorated with salamanders (his own emblem), fleurs-de-lys and the arms of France. These devices can be seen when the see-through page is turned over. Francis' bedroom, on the first floor of the tower (below), must have been one of the coldest rooms in the castle. Francis himself may have carved some graffiti near the window which reads 'Woman is fickle'.

BUILDING THE CHÂTEAU

Work on Chambord began in 1519. Some 20,000 workers spent 12 years building it before it was abandoned. The statistics of the building are breathtaking. Chambord is the largest château on the Loire. The front of the building is 128 metres long. There are 440 rooms and 365 fireplaces, each with its own chimney. There are over 80 staircases, one of which, in the centre of the château, is a wonderful double spiral staircase. It is thought to be based on a design by Leonardo da Vinci. Although the roof today has grey slates on, it was originally decorated with gilded lead. Around the château is a huge forest enclosed by a wall which, at 33 kilometres, is the longest in France.

1 **Bedroom of Francis I**
2 **'Cabinet' (study and chapel) of Francis I**
3 **Louis XIV's apartment**
4 **Bedroom of Marie Thérèse, wife of Louis XIV**
5 **Tapestry room containing scenes of Francis I hunting**
6 **Maurice de Saxe's drawing room**

INFLUENTIAL OWNERS

The château bears the stamp of some of the important people who lived or stayed there. The largest influence is that of Francis I, the builder, whose salamander emblem decorates many parts of the building. But he died in 1547, before some parts of the château, including the chapel, were completed. His son, Henry II, continued the work. Louis XIV (1638-1715), the most powerful king of France, created magnificent state apartments in the main part of the château. Other famous inhabitants included Stanislas, the exiled king of Poland, whose son-in-law, King Louis XV, ordered the chapel to be decorated, and Maurice de Saxe, one of Frances's most famous soldiers.

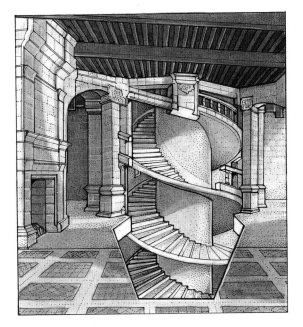

The two spirals of the great staircase wind, one above the other, round the same central shaft. This shaft is pierced with openings so that people on different staircases can see each other without ever meeting. This makes the staircase majestic and fun at the same time. The staircase rises through three large cross-shaped halls which were used for concerts and balls. The staircase is crowned by a lantern over 20 metres high. The top picture also shows one of four stoves that were installed in the cross-shaped room on the first floor by Maurice de Saxe.

7 **Hall made into a theatre by Maurice de Saxe**
8 **Guard room**
9 **Trophy room**
10 **Double spiral staircase**
11 **Louis XIV's billiard room**
12 **Corridor**
13 **Chapel, completed by Louis XV for King Stanislas**

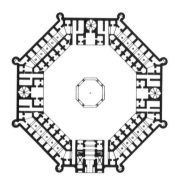

By the end of the Middle Ages, a great network of trade routes covered Europe and Asia. The merchants who travelled along these long and often dangerous routes, hundreds of miles from their own homes, needed safe places to stay.

CARAVANSERAI

Among the most impressive of these resting places for travellers were the 'caravanserai'. They were built throughout the Middle East from the 1200s. They not only provided a safe place to eat and sleep, but every conceivable service a weary traveller might need. They even became some travellers' homes for a while.

The caravanserai of Amīnābādh (above and left) was shaped like an octagonal fortress with a central well. The tall walls were defence against all but an army. The stables were placed around the inside wall, facing into the courtyard.

SMALL BEGINNINGS

The earliest caravanserai were simply walled enclosures protecting a well. Many caravanserai were built in the mountains, and were generally rather small and simple in design. They had a large central hall with arched aisles at the edges. A long bench running down the centre of the hall provided a sleeping or sitting place. Animals usually had to be left in stables outside the walls because there was rarely a central courtyard.

But gradually the caravanserai grew more important. The Seljuk rulers of Turkey built a large number of them. These greatly helped trade and brought great wealth to the country. By 1300, many caravanserai had grown into large buildings or even small communities. Just as many modern motels and hotels provide all the comforts of people's own homes, some of the caravanserai provided every conceivable service.

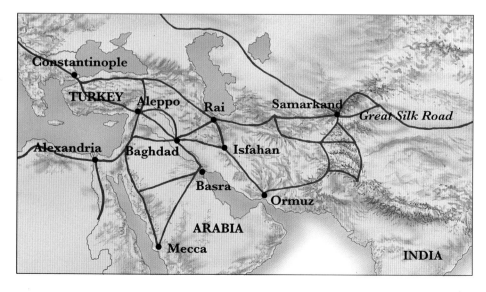

Constantinople
TURKEY · Aleppo · Rai · Samarkand · *Great Silk Road*
Alexandria · Baghdad · Isfahan
Basra · Ormuz
ARABIA
Mecca
INDIA

This map shows some of the main trade routes used by the Arab traders. The backbone of the system was the Great Silk Road which linked China with Europe.

LOCATION

Caravanserai were built either along highways or in towns, often a day's journey apart. Many caravanserai, especially in more remote areas, were like fortresses surrounded by walls and guarded by towers. Inside, the weary traveller might sleep on raised platforms in communal halls. In larger caravanserai there might be a second storey containing luxurious bedrooms or flat roofs where people could sleep.

The traveller might also find store-rooms where goods could be stowed safely, a dining room like a café, a washing fountain or bathhouse, a blacksmith and a leather worker who could repair damaged equipment, different sized stables for pack animals (such as camels, donkeys and mules) and for saddle animals such as horses. Each caravanserai was managed by a warden. Many of the services provided were free, paid for by the state.

Inside the walls, traders could rest, feed and water their animals and relax for a while. By travelling together in caravans, the traders protected themselves and each other from bandit attacks. Some caravans were very large and we know of several that contained over 5,000 camels.

TOWN CARAVANSERAI

Some caravanserai, especially those along the most important trade routes, were enormous. They had shops, bakeries, kitchens, refectories (dining halls), mosques and hospitals inside the walls. The huge caravanserai at Aliabad even had a flour mill and two ice houses in it!

Many of the caravanserai built in towns developed into important trading centres in their own right. These caravanserai were often built close to bazaars and were originally designed as depots. They had large warehouses where many different types of goods were stored in bales and packing-cases at their journey's end awaiting sale. Before long, the merchants who stayed in the caravanserai began to trade inside the caravanserai walls. As a result many of these caravanserai, which were sometimes called 'dars', grew into markets. Some became famous for selling particular goods, such as oil and soap.

This illustration made in about 1250 shows a caravan travelling to Mecca. The traders announce their progress with drums and trumpets.

A MAORI PA

During the first 1,000 years AD, the Polynesians settled on the islands of the Pacific. One of the last areas of the Pacific to be settled was what is now New Zealand. This was reached by the Maoris sometime during the 900s. The land must have seemed like a paradise for the first settlers, and they were able to build their homes wherever they wanted.

Maori houses often had roofs made from bundles of branches. These were laid on top of each other to form a type of waterproof thatch. The walls were made of panels of branches. Immediately below is a sleeping house. Bottom left is a larger house. Notice the earth bank along the side.

COMPETITION

Before the Maoris arrived, New Zealand's two islands had been uninhabited. The first settlers were able to live well by hunting and gathering food. But within a relatively short time, the settlers had hunted many of the animals close to extinction. As the stocks of animals shrank and the human population increased, so did competition for food. The Maoris began to develop agriculture and set about defending their food resources from other tribes.

HOMES FOR SAFETY

By about 1350, tribal warfare had become common in the North Island. The Maoris who lived there began to build their homes in easily defensible places. Favourite sites were in swamps, on rocky outcrops, and on the rims of extinct volcanoes. The Maoris improved the natural defences of the sites with earthworks, ditches and palisades (fences). In this way they created fortified villages, called 'pa', which were similar to the hill-forts built by Iron Age people in Europe. Some pa had very elaborate defences consisting of an interlocking maze of ditches and banks. In the centre of the pa was a palisade made of tree trunks, shaped into stakes with stone or obsidian tools. The stakes were sharpened and their tips hardened by fire. Inside the palisade was the main village which consisted of homes and storehouses.

SLEEPING HOUSES

We don't know very much about the houses which the Maoris built inside the pa. From archaeological evidence and by looking at other Maori villages, it seems likely that there were two types of building. The most common were small, squarish houses. From the remains of bedding material found inside them, such as twigs and leaves, it seems that many of the smaller houses were used as sleeping quarters.

LARGE HOUSES

Each pa also seems to have had at least one very large house in it. One of these large houses, found at Tiromoana pa in Hawke's Bay, was over 11 metres long and nearly 4 metres wide. This house had a pitched roof with a ridge held up by centre posts. The eaves of the roof were very long and overhung a low earth bank built along the base of the walls. This bank probably made the houses more weatherproof.

The main frame of these larger houses was made from poles, or sometimes planks, which must have been shaped from solid tree trunks with stone tools. The walls were made from small stakes and narrow planks. Some large houses had one or more hearth-pits dug in the earth floor.

CHIEFS

It seems likely that the large houses belonged to tribal chiefs. The size of each house may have indicated the power of the chief who lived in it. The houses naturally became used as places for assembly and discussion. We also know, from the diaries and log books of European sailors who went to New Zealand, that the large houses were used for receiving guests. It is probable that some of the houses may even have been specially built as guest houses for visitors. From eyewitness accounts it seems that many of the houses were richly decorated with carvings but, as yet, no examples have been found.

Many pa were similar to the one shown here. It is protected by a palisade of sharpened stakes and fighting platforms on which the defenders stood to hurl weapons.

Large houses were decorated with carvings (below). The carving on the far side of the door of this modern meeting house (far left) is a self-portrait of the carver.

ZULU HOMES

*A Zulu food pot. The Zulus'
staple foods were millet and
maize. These were ground into
flour on a concave stone and
made into porridge.*

The Zulu are an ancient people.
They are the descendants of a
wandering group of Bantu
people who lived by herding cattle
and farming. They settled in
Zululand in about AD 1000, long
before any European settlers came
to Africa. Their new homeland was
fertile, watered by several large
rivers, and free of the tsetse flies
which infected and killed livestock
in many other parts of Africa. The
Zulus had to fight to keep their
precious land. As a result, they
became one of the most powerful
and warlike nations in Africa.

A FAMILY HOME

The focus of Zulu life was the homestead
or 'umuzi', called a 'kraal' by the later
Afrikaaner settlers. The umuzi was
surrounded by a circular fence of thick
posts or brushwood and had three
entrances. In the centre of the umuzi was
an enclosure for penning cattle at night.

Each umuzi contained several huts,
each the home of a single family of parents
and their unmarried children. A headman,
called an 'induna', ruled the umuzi. The
induna's hut was always opposite the main
entrance of the umuzi. Around this were
grouped the huts of his wives arranged
according to seniority. The huts of his
unmarried sons were close to the entrance.

*Inside a Zulu hut, food is being
cooked over an open fire. The
furnishing of the hut is spartan,
with just a few mats on the
floor and pots for cooking
and storage.*

BEEHIVE HUTS

Each hut was built in the shape of a beehive. The framework was made from flexible saplings driven deeply into the ground and tied together with grass rope. Woven grass mats were then laid over the framework and fastened in place with grass ropes pulled over the top. The mats were overlapped to make the roof rainproof.

Each hut had an arched doorway. This was so low it had to be entered on hands and knees. It was closed by a removable door made from woven branches, which could be 'locked' by a pole lashed to the outside.

COOL HOMES

The grass thatch of the roof allowed some wind to pass right through the hut. This kept the interior of the hut cool, and blew away the smoke from the fireplace. The floor was made from cow dung and mud, often earth taken from the soil of an ant hill, mixed with water to make a kind of cement. When it had dried, the surface was polished with animal fat until it shone like marble.

> **'With cattle feeding solely on grass, the dung is merely a pulp which is practically odourless and soon dries out...This point is stressed because Europeans cannot understand why cow-dung is used... to smear frequently the earth-floors of huts, schools and churches.'**
>
> — *E. A. Ritter* —

FURNISHINGS

Inside the huts, there were very few furnishing. The Zulus slept on rush mats. Domestic items, such as sleeping mats and animal-skin blankets, pots and bags of tobacco, were hung from the sides of the hut when they were not being used.

Before eating, the Zulus washed their hands and faces in a special earthen basin. The families were arranged in strict order, the men on the right and the women on the left, with the eldest people nearest the door. Meals were eaten from a common food dish. Each person ate with his or her own wooden spoon which was placed with its handle on the floor and the bowl on the rim of the dish.

The umuzi was designed as both a fortified village and a cattle pen. Status was indicated by the position of the hut inside the umuzi. The huts of the most important people were farthest from the entrance. Cattle were the main wealth of the Zulus. In a region where wood is scarce, 'cakes' made of dried cow dung were used as fuel for the fires.

Stages in the construction of a Zulu hut (left to right). The design uses local building materials to produce a practical shelter. The Zulu men, who were warriors and cattle herders, built the huts. Women did everything else including cooking, cleaning, craftwork and most of the farming.

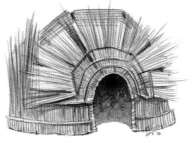

39

WEAVERS' COTTAGES

Before 1750, most goods, such as nails, shoes and woollen cloth, were made in rooms in workers' houses or in workshops in their back yards. The workers' houses were both their homes and workplaces.

CLOTH PRODUCTION

The cloth industry was typical of this method of production. In those days many people stayed at home to work and the whole family was involved in producing cloth. Different members of the family prepared the wool by carding (combing), spinning and weaving it by hand.

LOOM SHOPS

Weavers who kept their looms at home were called 'first hands'. Each weaver's cottage had spinning wheels and a loom for weaving. Since weaving was the most skilled job and the loom was the biggest piece of equipment, the needs of the weaver affected the design of the cottage.

1 Hearth
2 Raw wool
3 'Cards' for combing wool
4 Spinning wheel
5 Loom
6 Finished cloth ready for market

Many farmworkers and their families earned extra money by carding (combing), spinning and weaving in their homes (below). Wool merchants supplied the raw wool and collected the finished cloth to sell in their own shops or at nearby markets. Many merchants, who wanted their workers to live in the same area, built special cottages for them (right).

THE MAIN ROOMS

The weaver's loom was kept in a room called a loom shop. The loom shop could be bigger than all the bedrooms put together. Any spare rooms were rented out to other weavers. This meant that weavers' cottages were generally very crowded, so in many the children slept downstairs.

The house also had one or two bedrooms, a kitchen, a living room, a scullery and an outside privy. Houses did not have running water or bathrooms. Water had to be collected from the village pump or stream. Most people washed in the kitchen (which was the warmest room) using a jug and bowl, or in a wooden or tin bath. People cleaned their teeth with common salt or even brickdust. Soap was expensive, so crockery and cutlery were scrubbed with sand, brick dust and salt to get them clean.

HOUSEWORK

The cottages were very hard to keep clean. The wood or coal fires which heated them produced a huge amount of dust. Most cottages had bare floorboards or stone floors which needed regular sweeping with heather or twig brooms. Any rugs had to be taken outside and beaten to get rid of the dust or brushed with damp tea leaves which absorbed the dirt.

1 **Loom**
2 **Loom shop**
3 **Bedroom**
4 **Kitchen and dining room**
5 **Scullery**
6 **Larder**
7 **Privy**
8 **Passage between houses**

The cloth merchants who owned the weavers' cottages usually built them joined together in long rows, called terraces, to save money. The cottages were mostly two storeys high. The loom shop could be on any floor and always had very wide windows. This was to let plenty of light in so that the weavers could see their work clearly. The toilet, called a privy, was a small hut behind the cottage. The seat was made from wooden planks with a circle cut in them, placed over a bucket or a hole in the ground. The sewage might be spread on the land as fertilizer.

PORT SUNLIGHT

Many factory workers lived in squalid slums in industrial towns in the 19th century (below). Port Sunlight (bottom) was William Lever's attempt to build a new factory and provide the best possible living conditions for his employees. It is shown here in 1898, when only the factory and the first set of houses had been completed.

The rapid growth of towns during the Industrial Revolution brought a great increase in the number of squalid slum houses. In Britain, one rich industrialist, William Lever, felt it was his duty to improve the living conditions of his workers. When Lever ordered the building of a new soap factory in 1888, he also built a whole new village for them.

'It is my hope...to build houses in which our workpeople will be able to live and be comfortable. Semi-detached houses, with gardens back and front...they will learn that there is more enjoyment in life than in the mere going to and returning from work...'

— *William Lever* —

PLANNING PORT SUNLIGHT

Lever's architects designed not only houses for the workers to rent, but also a hospital, art gallery, gymnasium, swimming pool, theatre, and social clubs. Although this was unusual, many industrialists and architects before Lever had planned and built houses for their workers, and some had provided leisure facilities, too. But the houses had mostly been packed tightly into terraces, with few open spaces between. Port Sunlight was different because it combined good-quality industrial houses with pleasant open spaces.

THE HOUSES

The designs of the houses were very simple. The only unusual feature was that every house should have an internal bathroom. Two main designs were developed. The 'Kitchen Cottage' was the simplest, with a kitchen, scullery, larder and three bedrooms. The 'Parlour Cottage' was larger, with a parlour and a fourth bedroom.

The decoration of the earliest homes, built before 1890, is the simplest. Later houses had more complicated decoration, with moulded and twisted chimneys, carved woodwork and stone, pargeting (decorated plasterwork) and leaded windows. Lever said his architects had become 'more and more elaborate in architectural design, and more and more extravagent in the use of costly building materials'.

These are three-bedroomed 'Kitchen Cottages', with neat front gardens. Although actually built to similar designs, the houses in different blocks had distinctive external features which made them look very different to each other.

BLOCKS

Most of the houses were plainer. They were arranged in blocks consisting of between two and 18 cottages. Each house was built at least five metres from the nearest road, and all had front gardens. Each block enclosed a large space. Some of the space was divided into back yards where, hidden from public gaze, householders could hang their washing out to dry. Some of the space was made into allotments, which Lever believed were important. He even had some designed for children.

This scene shows the parlour in one of the larger cottages. Lever believed that badly-built houses soon became slums and that working people would be proud to live in and look after well-built homes. Port Sunlight was an experiment which proved this idea to be correct.

UNUSUAL DESIGNS

Two unusual designs were cottages that looked like the birthplace of the playwright William Shakespeare, and others that looked like a timber-framed hall.

There had also been plans to build houses in styles representing the countries in which Lever's company had factories. However, only one such block was built, in a Flemish style using Belgian bricks.

A MODEL ESTATE

Port Sunlight caused a sensation. The estate received a flood of distinguished visitors, including the king and queen. Originally there were 28 houses. The village now contains 850 houses, as well as 72 flats and maisonettes, which are still occupied. During its history Port Sunlight has been constantly modernized with the installation of electricity, gas and many other improvements. The design of the village, particularly its emphasis on well-built houses standing in green spaces, has greatly influenced town planning throughout the 20th century.

A 'New Rapid' geyser (water heater) of 1884 similar to geysers fitted in some houses at Port Sunlight. Running hot water was found mainly in the homes of the very rich and was a real luxury for working people.

BIOSPHERE 2

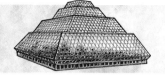

Thousands of square metres of glass enclose Biosphere 2's seven environments. These include an ocean with a coral reef, a river, a rainforest, a marsh, savannah, a desert and living quarters for the humans who live inside.

High on a plateau in the Arizona desert in the USA sits what is perhaps the most unusual and expensive home on earth. The building, which is made mainly of glass and steel, covers 3.15 acres and cost over $150 million.

SEALED INSIDE

Biosphere 2 is a giant laboratory built to discover how the ecosystem of the earth works and to study the problems of colonizing outer space. It is a completely airtight, self-contained environment. Once inside, the eight people who lived in it for two years had to produce their own food. They even relied on the interaction of the plants and animals in the Biosphere to produce enough oxygen for them to breathe.

One of the Biospherians harvesting rice in the agricultural biome - one of the seven environments enclosed inside Biosphere 2.

BUILDING MATERIALS

Biosphere 2 looks like a gigantic greenhouse. It is made of a steel space frame covered in glass panels which are glued in place to make the building airtight. The series of buildings which make up the Biosphere stand on thick concrete foundations. A special lining and a massive underground tray made of stainless steel prevent air and water inside the buildings from escaping through the ground.

All the materials used in the Biosphere had to be free of toxic substances which might pollute the sensitive ecosystem. All metal surfaces, for example, were painted with polyester resins to prevent pollution of the environment inside.

SELF-SUFFICIENCY

The closed environment of the Biosphere was intended to be a kind of 20th century 'Noah's Ark'. It was planned that each of the small environments would be self-sufficient. Each part would also help to maintain life in the other parts. People and plants would exchange oxygen and carbon dioxide, and wastes would be used as fertilizers. Damp air from the ocean area would provide moisture for the swamp, and plants and animals would be food for each other.

ENVIRONMENTS

Biosphere 2 houses over 3,800 plant and animal species in seven separate ecological areas, or 'biomes'. These represent the main natural environments found on Biosphere 1, the earth. The human biome contained an observatory, a library, a communications centre with telephone and computer connections to the outside world, a gym, a dining hall, and eight separate 34-metre-square sleeping apartments, all housed inside a white dome. The four male and four female Biospherians were sealed inside Biosphere 2 for two years. While they lived inside the Biosphere they farmed the land in the agricultural biome and performed a great variety of scientific experiments.

ARTIFICIAL WEATHER

The Biosphere was not large enough to have natural weather inside it, so machines helped to simulate this. Over 3,500 sensors feed data to the computer-controlled heaters and coolers which balance the temperature and the pumps which direct the flow of water and air around the buildings. A giant pair of rubber lungs help to equalize the air pressure in different parts of the Biosphere to prevent the glass walls exploding or imploding.

PROBLEMS

On 27 September 1993 eight pale and thin people emerged from the Biosphere. During their two-year stay in the ecosystem they had all lost weight and had had to deal with many problems. The plants were unable to produce enough oxygen, and sometimes air had to be pumped in from outside to keep the people and animals alive. Insects ate many of the crops. Some of the animals, including the bees and hummingbirds, died. Some of the Biospherians became ill, suffering from skin diseases among other illnesses.

LESSONS FOR THE FUTURE

In spite of these setbacks, Biosphere 2 did support eight humans and several thousands of other species. The recycling systems worked well. Although receiving some criticism, the project has helped us understand better how humans might live in closer harmony with nature. Perhaps it can teach us how to build better homes in the future or even make the colonization of outer space a more practical possibility.

Mealtime in the Biosphere. This is a typical meal eaten by the Biospherians during the two-year experiment.

KEY DATES AND GLOSSARY

This list of key dates includes some of the major inventions and developments in the methods humans have used to make their homes. Dates before AD 1400 are approximate.

BC

25,000 Stone Age artists paint inside their caves. People take first steam baths by throwing water over rocks heated in a fire.

24,000 Hut-building is a well-established skill. The first huts are lean-tos with skin and brushwood supported on branches.

14,000 Round, stone-walled huts with sunken floors become common in the Middle East. Square hide-covered huts are built in South America.

7,000 Wattle and daub (mud plastered on woven branches) becomes a common building material in Europe.

6,000 The Chinese build round wooden huts with sunken floors.

4,000 The first known building with decorated walls is built in Mesopotamia.

3,000 Large communal meeting houses built in China out of wood and thatch.

3,000 The first high-backed chairs used in Egypt. Ancient Egyptians also invent the bathroom and a form of concrete (by using gypsum to bind stone and brick).

2,000 The first door lock made near Nineveh in Assyria.

1,200 Pacific islanders build wooden houses on stilts close to the shoreline.

150 Romans discover that volcanic dust found near Vesuvius sets hard when mixed with lime and water. They call it *cementium*. The Romans also mass-produce fired bricks; invent central heating (the hypocaust); and invent the rounded arch.

AD

250 The squinch is invented in the Middle East. This allows domed roofs to be built more easily.

1463 The first reported numbering of houses introduced in Paris.

1589 The first flushing lavatory is invented by Sir John Harrington.

1716 Hot water central heating invented by Martin Triewald, a Swedish engineer.

1799 First gas fire demonstrated in France.

1824 Joseph Aspidin patents modern synthetic cement.

1885 The world's first skyscraper, the 10-storey Chicago Home Insurance Building, erected.

Tipis are the traditional homes of the Plains Indians of North America. They are made of a buffalo hide cover over a frame of strong poles. They were designed to be put up and taken down quickly, so that the tribe could follow the herds. The Indians hung their possessions, weapons and medicine bags inside the tipi around the walls. Smoke flaps at the top of the tipi could be closed to keep the heat in or opened to let the smoke of the fire out.

Glossary

allotments: small plots of public land that people can grow food or flowers on.

bitumen: a naturally occurring tarry substance.

citadel: a fortress overlooking a city.

Cro-Magnons: a type of prehistoric human who lived in Europe, Asia and Africa from about 35,000 to 8,000 BC.

dormer window: window projecting from a sloping roof.

eaves: the overhanging edges of a roof.

foundations: the base of a building, usually under the ground, which is designed to carry the building's weight.

gable: the triangular upper part of a wall at the end of a ridged roof.

Ice Age: a period when ice sheets cover large regions of the earth. Ice Ages occur periodically. The last Ice Age began about 1¾ million years ago.

lantern: a construction, with windows, that covers a room or dome.

Neanderthals: prehistoric humans who lived in Europe, Africa and Asia from about 100,000 to 35,000 years ago.

obsidian: a kind of natural glass formed by volcanoes.

pargeting: ornamental plasterwork.

quern: a handmill for grinding grain into flour.

relief: a panel with a carving on it.

skyscraper: a building built around, and whose weight is carried by, a steel frame.

This allows the building to be many storeys higher than one whose weight is carried by walls.

squinch: a half-dome built across the corner of a square chamber to make it octagonal. This allows a dome to be more easily built over it.

Stone Age: the period during which people used stone tools. The Stone Age began about 2.5 million years ago. About 3,000 BC, bronze tools were developed in the Middle East.

terracotta: hard, unglazed pottery which is usually brownish-red in colour.

wattle and daub: a building material made from panels of woven thin branches plastered with mud or a similar substance.

Quotations

The marriage blessing is based on Indian inscriptions dating from shortly after the fall of Mohenjo-Daro. The Egyptian inscription is one of many pieces of 'wise advice' from ancient Egypt. During his life (about AD 55-138), Juvenal was a soldier, a priest and a lawyer. He is most famous for his *Satires* - writings which made vicious attacks on corruption and the follies of ancient Rome. E. A. Ritter grew up among the Zulus in Natal. The description comes from his book *Shaka's Zulu*, published by Greenhill Books. Victorian industrialist William Lever (1851-1925) became rich through manufacturing and selling soap.

INDEX